THE
SPEÉCH

OF

VILLIAM WILBERFORCE, Esq.

REPRESENTATIVE

FOR THE

COUNTY OF YORK,

ON

WEDNESDAY THE 13TH OF MAY, 1789,

ON THE QUESTION OF THE

ABOLITION OF THE SLAVE TRADE.

TO WHICH ARE ADDED,

THE RESOLUTIONS THEN MOVED,

AND

A SHORT SKETCH

OF THE

SPEECHES OF THE OTHER MEMBERS.

———

LONDON:

PRINTED AT THE Logographic Press,

AND SOLD BY

J WALTER, No 169, PICCADILLY; C STALKER, STATIONERS-COURT,
LUDGATE-STREET; AND W. RICHARDSON, UNDER THE ROYAL-
EXCHANGE.

T H E

S P E E C H

OF

WILLIAM WILBERFORCE, Esq.

Sir William Dolben *,

WHEN I confider the magnitude of the
subject which I am to bring before
the House—a fubject, in which the interefts, not of this country, nor of Europe
alone, but of the whole world, and of pof-
terity, are involved; and when I think, at
the fame time, on the weaknefs of the ad-
vocate who has undertaken this great caufe
—when thefe reflections prefs upon my
mind, it is impoffible for me not to feel both
terrified and concerned at my own inadequacy
to fuch a tafk. But when I reflect, however,
on the encouragement which I have had,

* Chairman of the Committee.

A 2   through

through the whole courfe of a long and la-
borious examination of this queftion, how
much candour I have experienced, and how
conviction has increafed within my own
mind, in proportion as I have advanced in
my labours ;—when I reflect, efpecially,
that, however adverfe any Gentlemen may
now be, yet we fhall all, moft affuredly, be
of one opinion in the end. When I turn
myfelf to thefe thoughts, I take courage—I
determine to forget all my other fears, and
I march forward with a firmer ftep, in the
full affurance that my caufe will bear me
out, and that I fhall be able to juftify, upon
the cleareft principles, every refolution in
my hand—the avowed end of which, Sir,
is,—the total Abolition of the Slave Trade.

I wifh exceedingly, in the outfet, to
guard both myfelf and the Houfe from entering into the fubject with any fort of paffion. It is not their paffions I fhall appeal
to—I afk only for their cool and impartial
reafon ; and I wifh not to take them by fur-
prize, but to deliberate, point by point,
upon every part of this queftion. I mean
not

not to accufe any one, but to take the fhame upon myfelf, in common, indeed, with the whole Parliament of Great Britain, for having fuffered this horrid trade to be carried on, under their authority. We are all guilty—we ought all to plead guilty, and not to exculpate ourfelves, by throwing the blame on others.; and I therefore deprecate every kind of reflection, againft the various defcriptions of people who are more immediately involved in this wretched bufinefs.

In opening the nature of the Slave Trade, I need only obferve, that it is found, by experience, to be juft fuch as every man, who ufes his reafon, would infallibly conclude it to be. For my own part, fo clearly am I convinced of the mifchiefs infeparable from it, that I fhould hardly want any further evidence than my own mind would furnifh, by the moft fimple deductions. Facts, however, are now laid before the Houfe. A report has been made by his Majefty's Privy Council, which, I truft, every Gentleman has read, and which afcertains the Slave Trade to be juft fuch in practice as we know,

from

from theory, that it muſt be. What ſhould
we ſuppoſe muſt naturally be the conſe-
quence of our carrying on a Slave Trade
with Africa? With a country, vaſt in its
extent, not utterly barbarous, but civilized
in a very ſmall degree? Does any one ſuppoſe a Slave Trade would *help* their civilization? That Africa would *profit* by ſuch
an intercourſe? Is it not plain, that ſhe muſt
ſuffer from it? That civilization muſt be
checked; that her barbarous manners muſt
be made more barbarous; and that the happineſs of her millions of inhabitants muſt
be prejudiced by her intercourſe with Britain? Does not every one ſee, that a Slave
Trade, carried on around her coaſts, muſt
carry violence and deſolation to her very
centre? That, in a Continent, juſt emer-
ging from barbariſm, if a Trade in Men is
eſtabliſhed—if her men are all converted
into goods, and become commodities that
can be bartered, it follows, they muſt be
ſubject to ravage juſt as goods are; and this
too, at a period of civilization, when there
is no protecting Legiſlature to defend this
their only ſort of property, in the ſame

manner

manner as the rights of property are maintained by the legiflature of every civilized country.

We fee then, in the nature of things, how eafily all the practices of Africa are to be accounted for. Her kings are never compelled to war, that we can hear of, by public principles,—by national glory——ftill lefs by the love of their people. In Europe it is the extenfion of commerce, the maintenance of national honor, or fome great public object, that is ever the motive to war with every monarch; but, in Africa, it is the perfonal *avarice* and *fenfuality* of their kings: thefe two vices of avarice and fenfuality, (the moft powerful and predominant in natures thus corrupt) we tempt, we ftimulate in all thefe African Princes; and we depend upon thefe vices for the very maintenance of the Slave Trade. Does the king of Barbeffin want brandy * ? He has only to fend his troops, in the night-time, to burn and defolate a village; the captives will ferve as commodities, that may be bartered with the Britifh trader. What a

* Vide Dr. Spaarman's evidence before the Privy Council.

ftriking

ſtriking view of the wretched ſtate of Africa does the tragedy of Calabar furniſh !
Two towns, formerly hoſtile, had ſettled
their differences, and by an inter-marriage
among their chiefs, had each pledged themſelves to peace; but the Trade in Slaves was
prejudiced by ſuch pacifications, and it became, therefore, the policy of our traders
to renew the hoſtilities. This, their policy,
was ſoon put in practice, and the ſcene of
carnage which followed was ſuch, that it is
better, perhaps, to refer Gentlemen to the
Privy Council's Report, than to agitate
their minds by dwelling on it.

The Slave Trade, in its very nature, is
the ſource of ſuch kind of tragedies, nor
has there been a ſingle perſon, almoſt, before the Privy Council, who does not add
ſomething, by his teſtimony, to the maſs
of evidence upon this point. Some, indeed,
of theſe Gentlemen, and particularly the
Delegates from Liverpool, have endeavoured to reaſon down this plain principle ; ſome
have palliated it, but there is not one, I believe, who does not, more or leſs, admit it.

Some

Some, nay moſt, I believe, have admitted the Slave Trade to be the chief cauſe of wars in Africa. Mr. Penny * has called it the *concurrent* cauſe—ſome confeſs it to be *ſometimes* the cauſe ; but argue, that it can-not often be ſo.——Here I muſt make one obſervation, which, I hope, may be done, without offence to any one, and which I do, once for all, though it applies equally to many other evidences upon this ſubject. I mean to lay it down, as my principle, that evidences, and eſpecially *intereſted* evidences, are not to be the judges of the *argument*. In matters of *faćt*, of which they ſpeak, I admit their competency ; I mean not to ſuſpect their credibility, with reſpect to any thing they ſee or hear, or themſelves perſonally know ; but, in reaſoning about *cauſes and effećts*, I hold them them to be to-tally incompetent. So far, therefore, from ſubmitting to their concluſions, in this re-ſpect, I utterly diſcard them. I take their premiſes readily and fairly ; but, *upon* theſe premiſes, I muſt judge for myſelf: and the

* Liverpool Delegate.

Houſe,

Houfe, I truft——nay, I perfectly well
know, will, in like manner judge for itfelf.
Confident affertions, therefore, not of facts,
but of the *fuppofed confequences* of facts, however preffed by the Liverpool Delegates, or
any other interefted perfons, go for nothing
in my eftimation; and it is neceffary that Parliament fhould proceed upon this principle;
as well in this as every other public queftion, in which interefted evidences muft be
examined. Thus the African Committee
have reported, that very few enormities, *in
their opinion*, can have been practifed in Africa; becaufe, in forty years, only two complaints have been made to them. I admit
the fact to them undoubtedly; but, I truft,
Gentlemen will judge for themfelves, whether Parliament is to reft fatisfied that there
are no abufes in Africa, in fpite of all the
pofitive proofs of fo many witneffes on the
fpot to the contrary. Whether, for inftance, Mr. Wadftrom's evidence, Dr.
Spaarman's, Captain Hill's, are to go for
nothing, many of whom, either faw the
battles, were told by the kings themfelves,
that it was for the fake of flaves they went
to

to battle, or conversed with a variety of prisoners taken by these very means. In truth, an enquiry from the African Committee whether any foul play prevails in Africa, is somewhat like an application to the Custom-house officers, to know whether any smuggling is going on; the officer may tell you, that very few seizures are made, and very few frauds come to his knowledge; but does it follow, that Parliament must agree to all the *reasonings* of the officer; and, though smuggling be ever so notorious throughout the land, must agree there is no smuggling, because the officer reports that he makes very few seizures, and seldom hears of it? I will not believe, therefore, the *mere opinions* of African traders, concerning the nature and consequences of the slave trade. It is a trade in *its principle* most inevitably calculated to spread disunion among the African princes, to sow the seeds of every mischief, to inspire enmity, to destroy humanity; and it is found *in practice*, by the most abundant testimony, to have had the effect in Africa of carrying misery, devastation, and ruin

wherever

wherever its baneful influence has ex-
tended.

Having now difpofed of the firft part of
this fubject, I muft fpeak of the *tranfit of
the flaves in the Weft Indies.*

This, I confefs, in my own opinion, is
the moft wretched part of the whole fubject.
So much mifery condenfed in fo little room, is
more than the human imagination had ever
before conceived. I will not accufe the Liverpool merchants : I will allow them—nay,
I will believe them to be men of humanity ;
and I will therefore believe, if it were not
for the multitude of thefe wretched objects,
if it were not for the enormous magnitude
and extent of the evil which diftracts their
attention from individual cafes, and makes
them think generally, and therefore lefs
feelingly on the fubject, they never would
have perfifted in the trade. I verily believe,
therefore, if the wretchednefs of any *one* of
the many hundred negroes ftowed in each
fhip could be brought before their view, and
remain within the fight of the African mer-
chant,

chant, that there is no one among them, whofe
heart would bear it ?—Let any one imagine
to himfelf, 6 or 700 of thefe wretches chain-
ed two and two, furrounded with every object that is naufeous and difgufting, dif-
eafed. and ftruggling under every kind of
wretchednefs !—How can we bear to think
of fuch a fcene as this ? One would think
it had been determined to heap upon them
all the varieties of bodily pain, for the pur-
pofe of blunting the feelings of their mind ;
and yet, in this very point (to fhew the
power of human prejudice), the fituation of
the flaves has been defcribed by Mr. Norris,
one of the Liverpool delegates, in a manner
which, I am fure, will convince the Houfe
how intereft can draw a film over the eyes,
fo thick, that total blindnefs could do no
more, and how it is our duty, therefore, to
truft not to the reafonings of interefted men,
or to their way of colouring a tranfaction.

" Their *apartments*," fays Mr. Norris,
" are *fitted up* as much for their advantage
as circumftances will admit." The right
ancle of one indeed is *connected* with the left
ancle of another *by a fmall iron fetter*, and, if
they

they are turbulent, by another on their wrifts. " They have feveral meals a-day ; fome," as he tells you, " of *their own country provifions, with the beft fauces of African cookery* ; and. by way of variety, another meal of pulfe, &c. according to European tafte. After breakfaft they have water to wafh themfelves, while their apartments are perfumed with frankincenfe and lime-juice. Before dinner, they are amufed after the manner of their country. The fong and the dance are *promoted*;" and, as if the whole was really a fcene of pleafure and diffipation, it is added, that games of chance are furnifhed. " The men play and fing, while the women and girls make fanciful ornaments with beads, which they are plentifully fupplied with." Such is the fort of ftrain in which the Liverpool Delegates, and particularly Mr. Norris, gave evidence before the Privy Council.

What will the Houfe think, when, by the concurring teftimony of other witneffes, the true hiftory is laid open. The flaves, who are fometimes defcribed as rejoicing at their captivity, are fo wrung with mifery

at

at leaving their country, that it is the conftant practice to *fet fail in the night*, left they
fhould be fenfible of their departure. The
pulfe which Mr. Norris talks of are *horfe
beans*; and the fcantinefs, both of water
and provifion, was fuggefted by the very
legiflature of Jamaica, in the report of their
Committee, to be a fubject that called for
the interference of Parliament. Mr. Norris talks of frankincenfe and lime-juice;
when all the furgeons tell you, the flaves are
ftowed fo clofe, that there is not room to
tread among them : and when you have it
in evidence from Sir George Yonge, that
even in a fhip which wanted 200 of her com-
plement, *the ftench was intolerable*. The fong
and the dance, fays Mr. Norris, are *promoted*.
It had been more fair, perhaps, if he had
explained that word *promoted*. The truth
is, that, for the fake of exercife, thefe mi-
ferable wretches, loaded with chains, op-
preffed with difeafe and wretchednefs, are
forced to dance by the terror of the lafh,
and fometimes by the actual ufe of it. " I,"
fays one of the other evidences, " was employed to dance the men, while another
                                    perfon

person danced the women." Such then is
the meaning of the word *promoted*; and it
may be obferved too, with refpect to food,
that an inftrument is fometimes carried out,
in order to force them to eat, which is the
fame fort of proof how much they enjoy
themfelves in that inftance alfo. As to their
finging; what fhall we fay, when we are
told, that their fongs are fongs of lamenta-
tion upon their departure, which, while
they fing, they are always in tears, info-
much that one Captain (more humane, as I
fhould conceive him, therefore, than the
reft) threatened one of the women with a
flogging, becaufe the mournfulnefs of her
fong was too painful for his feelings.

In order, however, not to truft too much
to any fort of defcription, I will call the attention of the Houfe to one fpecies of evidence, which is abfolutely infallible. Death
at leaft, is a fure ground of evidence, and
the proportion of deaths will not only con-
firm, but, if poffible, will even aggravate
our fufpicion of their mifery in the tranfit.
It will be found, upon an average of all the
fhips of which evidence has been given at
the

the Privy Council, that exclufive of thofe who perifh before they fail, not lefs than 12½ per cent. perifh in the paffage. Befides thefe, the Jamaica report tells you, that not lefs than 4½ per cent. die on fhore before the day of fale, which is only a week or two from the time of landing. One third more die in the feafoning, and this in a country exactly like their own, where they are healthy and happy, as fome of the evidences would pretend. The difeafes, however, which they contract on fhipboard, the aftrin-gent wafhes which are to hide their wounds, and the mifchievous tricks ufed to make make them up for fale, are, as the Jamaica report fays, (a moft precious and valuable re-port, which I fhall often have to advert to) one principal caufe of this mortality. Upon the whole, however, here is a mortality of about 50 per cent, and this among negroes who are not bought unlefs quite healthy at firft, and unlefs (as the phrafe is with cat-tle), they are found in wind and limb.

How then can the Houfe refufe its belief to the multiplied teftimonies, before the

B   Privy

privy Council, of the savage treatment of
. the Negroes in the middle paffage ?—Nay,
indeed, what need is there of any evidence?
The number of deaths fpeaks for itfelf, and
makes all fuch enquiry, fuperfluous.

As foon as ever I had arrived thus far in
my inveftigation of the Slave Trade, I confefs to you, Sir, fo enormous, fo dreadful,
fo irremediable did its wickednefs appear,
that my own mind was completely made up
for the abolition. A Trade founded in iniquity, and carried on as this was, muft be
abolifhed, let the Policy be what it might,—
let the confequences be what they would,
I from this time determined that I would
never reft till I had effected its abolition.—
Such enormities as thefe having once come
within my knowledge, I fhould not have
been faithful to the fight of my eyes, to the
ufe of my fenfes and my reafon, if I had
fhrunk from attempting the abolition; It is
true, indeed, my mind was harraffed beyond
meafure; for when Weft India Planters and
Merchants retorted it upon me, that it was
the British Parliament had authorized this

Trade ;

Trade; when they faid to me, " It is *your* Acts of Parliament,—it is *your* encouragement,—it is faith in *your laws*, in *your* protection, that has tempted us into this Trade, and has now made it neceffary to us :" It became difficult, indeed, what to anfwer ; if the ruin of the Weft Indies threatened us on the one hand, while this load of wickednefs preffed upon us on the other, the alternative, indeed, was awful.

It naturally fuggefted itfelf to me, how ftrange it was that providence, however myfterious in its ways, fhould fo have conftituted the world, as to make one part of it depend for its exiftence on the depopulation and devaftation of another.

I could not, therefore, help diftrufting the arguments of thofe, who infifted that the plundering of Africa, was neceffary for the cultivation of the Weft Indies. I could not believe that the fame Being who forbid rapine and bloodfhed, had made rapine and bloodfhed neceffary to the well-being of any

B 2   part

part of his univerſe. I felt a confidence in
this principle, and took the reſolution to
act upon it : ſoon indeed the light broke
in upon me ; the ſuſpicion of my mind
was every day confirmed by encreaſing in-
for mation, the truth became clear, the
evidence I have to offer upon this point, is
now deciſive and compleat ; and I wiſh to
obſerve, with ſubmiſſion, but with perfect
conviction of heart, what an inſtance is this
how ſafely we may truſt the rules of juſtice,
the dictates of conſcience, and the laws of
God, in oppoſition even to the ſeeming impolicy of theſe eternal principles.

I hope now to prove, by authentic evidence, that in truth the Weſt Indies have
nothing to fear from the total and immediate abolition of the Slave Trade : I will enter
minutely into this point, and, I do intreat the
moſt exact attention of gentlemen moſt intereſted in this part of the queſtion ; the reſo-
lutions I have to offer are many and particular, for the purpoſe of bringing each
point under a ſeparate, diſcuſſion ; and thus
I hope

I hope it will be fhewn, that Parliament is not difpofed to overlook the interefts of the Weft Indies.

The principle, however, upon which I found the neceffity of abolition is *not Policy* but *Juftice*,—but though juftice be the principle of the meafure, yet, I truft, I fhall diftinctly prove it to be reconcileable with our trueft political intereft.

In entering, therefore, into the next branch of my fubject, namely, *the ftate of flaves in the Weft Indies*, I would obferve, that here, as in many other cafes, it happens that the owner or principal, generally fends out the beft orders imaginable, which the manager upon the fpot may purfue or not, as he pleafes. I do not accufe even the manager of any native cruelty, he is a perfon made like ourfelves (for nature is much the fame in all perfons) but it is *habit* that generates cruelty :—This man looking down upon his Slaves as a fet of Beings of another nature from himfelf, can have no fympathy for them, and it is fympathy, and nothing elfe

B 3   than

than sympathy, which according to the best writers and judges of the subject, is the true spring of humanity. Let us ask then what are the causes of the mortality in the West Indies :—

In the first place, the *disproportion of sexes;* an evil, which, when the Slave Trade is abolished, must in the course of nature cure itself.

In the second place, *the disorders contracted in the middle passage :* and here let me touch upon an argument for ever used by the advocates for the Slave Trade, the fallacy of which is no where more notorious than in this place.

It is said to be the *interest* of the traders to use their slaves well : the astringent washes, escarotics, and mercurial ointments by which they are made up for sale, is one answer to this argument. In this instance it is not their interest to use them well ; and although in some respects self-interest and humanity will go together, yet unhappily

through

through the whole progrefs of the Slave
Trade, the very converfe of this principle is
continually occuring.

A third caufe of deaths in the Weft
Indies is *excessive labour joined with impro-*
per food. I mean not to blame the Weft
Indians, for this evil fprings from the very
nature of things ;—in this country the work
is fairly paid for, and diftributed among our
labourers, according to the reafonablenefs
of things ; and if a trader or manufacturer
finds his profits decreafe, he retrenches his
own expences, he leffens the number of his
hands, and every branch of trade finds its
proper level. In the Weft Indies the whole
number of Slaves remains with the fame
mafter,—is the mafter pinched in his profits ? The flave allowance is pinched in confequence; for as charity begins at home, the
ufual gratification of the mafter will never
be given up, fo long as there is a poffibility
of making the retrenchment from the allowance of the flaves. There is, therefore,
a conftant tendency to the very minimum
with refpect to flaves allowance ; and
if in any one hard year the flaves get
through upon a reduced allowance, from the

B 4   very

very nature of man it muſt happen, that this, becomes a precedent upon other occaſions ; nor is the gradual deſtruction of the ſlave a conſideration ſufficient to counteract the immediate advantage and profit that is got by their hard uſage. Here then we perceive again, how the argument of intereſt fails alſo with reſpect to the treatment of ſlaves in the Weſt Indies. Intereſt is undoubtedly the great ſpring of action in the affairs of mankind ; but it is *immediate* and *preſent,* not *future* and *diſtant* intereſt, however real, that is apt to actuate us. We may truſt that men will follow their intereſt when preſent impulſe and intereſt correſpond, but not otherwiſe. That this is a true obſervation may be proved by every thing in life.—Why do we make laws to puniſh men ? It is their intereſt to be upright and virtuous, without theſe laws : but there is a preſent impulſe continually breaking in upon their better judgment; an impulſe contrary to their permanent and known intereſt, which it is not even in the power of all our laws ſufficiently to refrain. It is ridiculous to ſay, therefore, that men will be bound by their intereſt, when preſent

gain

gain or when the force of paffion is urging them : It is no lefs ridiculous than if we were to fay that a ftone cannot be thrown into the air, nor any body move along the earth, becaufe the great principle of gravitation muft keep them for ever faft. The principle of gravitation is true ; and yet in fpite of it there are a thoufand motions which bo dies may be driven into continually, and upon which we ought as much to reckon as on gravitation itfelf. This principle, therefore, of felf-intereft, which is brought in to anfwer every charge of cruelty throughout the Slave Trade, is not to be thus generally admitted. That the allowance is too fhort in the Weft Indies appears very plain alfo from the evidence ; the allowance in the prifons I conceive muft be an under allowance, and yet I find it to be fomewhat lefs than this : Dr. ADAIR (who is not very favourable to my propofitions, and who by way of evidence wrote a fort of pamphlet againft me to the Privy Council) has faid that even *he* thinks their food at crop-time too little ; and I obferve from Governor ORD's ftatement that he ac-

counts

counts for their being more healthy at a lefs favourable feafon of the year, from: their being better fed at the unfavourable feafon.

Another caufe of the mortality of flaves is, the dreadful diffolutenefs of their manners. Here it might be faid, that felf-intereft muft induce the planters to wifh for fome order and decency around their families ; but in this cafe alfo, it is flavery itfelf that is the mifchief. Slaves, confider-. ed as cattle, left without inftruction, with-out any inftitution of marriage, fo depreffed as to have no means almoft of civilization, will undoubtedly be diffolute; and, until attempts are made to raife them a little above their prefent fituation, this fource of mortality will remain.

. Some evidences indeed have endeavoured to difprove that there is any particular wretchednefs among the flaves in the Weft Indies. Admiral Barrington tells you, he has feen them look fo happy, that he has fometimes wifhed himfelf one of them. I conceive that, in a cafe like this, an Admiral's ral's evidence is perhaps the very worſt that can be taken. It is as if a King were to judge of the private happineſs of his ſoldiers by ſeeing them on a review day. The ſight of the Admiral would no doubt exhilerate ·their· faces; he would ſee them in their béſt clothes, and they, perhaps, might hope for a few of the crumbs which fell from the Admiral's table; but does it follow that there is no hard treatment of ſlaves·in the Weſt Indies? The Admiral's wiſh to be one of theſe ſlaves himſelf, proves perhaps that he was in an odd humour at the moment, or perhaps it might mean (for all the world knows his humanity), that he could wiſh to alleviate their ſufferings, by taking a ſhare upon himſelf; but at leaſt it proves nothing of their general treatment; and, at any rate, it is but a negative proof which affects not the other evidences to the contrary.

It is now to be remarked, that *all* theſe cauſes of mortality among the ſlaves do undoubtedly admit of a remedy, and it is the
abolition

abolition of the flave trade that will ferve as this remedy. When the manager fhall know, that a frefh importation is not to be had from Africa, and that he cannot retrieve the deaths he occafions by any new purchafes, humanity muft be introduced ; an improvement in the fyftem of treating them will thus infallibly be effected, an affiduous care of their health and of their morals, marriage inftitutions, and many other things, as yet little thought of, will take place ; becaufe they will be abfolutely neceffary.

Births will thus encreafe naturally ; inftead of frefh acceffions of the fame negroes from Africa, each generation will then improve upon the former, and thus will the Weft Indies themfelves eventually profit by the abolition of the Slave Trade.

But, Sir, I will fhew by experience already had, how the multiplication of flaves depends upon their good treatment. All fides agree, that flaves are much better treated ed now than they were thirty years ago in the Weſt Indies, and that there is every day a growing improvement.

I will ſhew, therefore, by authentic do-cuments, how their numbers have encreaſed (or rather how the decreaſe has leſſened), in the ſame proportion as the treatment has improved.

There were in Jamaica, in the year 1761, 147,000 ſlaves; in the year 1787, there were 256,000; in all this period of 26 years, 165,000 were imported, which would be upon an average 2150 per annum, there being, on an average of the whole 26 years, 1 1-15th per cent. yearly diminution of the number of ſlaves on the iſland.

In fact, however, I find that the diminu-tion in the firſt period, when they were the worſt uſed, was $2\frac{1}{4}$ per cent. in the next 7 years it was 1 per cent. and the average of the laſt period is 3-5ths per cent. It ſhould alſo be obſerved, that there has lately been, on account of the war, a much more

than

than ordinary diminution, which was the cafe alfo in the former war, befides that 15,000 have been deftroyed by the late famine and hurricanes. Upon thefe premifes I ground a conclufion, that in Jamaica there is at this time an actual encreafe of population among the flaves begun. It may fairly be prefumed, that fince the year 1782 this has been the cafe, and that the births by this time exceed the deaths by about 1000 or 1100 per annum. It is true, the fexes are not altogether equal; but this difference is fo fmall, that if the proper number of women were added, the births to be expected in confequence would be no more than 300 per annum, which fhews this to be a matter of little confequence.

In the ifland of Barbadoes the cafe is nearly the fame as at Jamaica.

In St. Chriftophers, there are 9600 females, and 10,300 males; fo that an increafe by birth, if the treatment is tolerable, may fairly be expected.

In Dominica, Governor Ord writes, that there is a natural increase, though it is yet inconsiderable, and though the smuggling in that island makes it not appear so favourably.

In Nevis there are absolutely five women to four men.

In Antigua, the epidemical disorders have lately cut off 1-4th or 1-5th of the negroes; but this cannot be expected to return, especially when the grand cause of epidemical disorders is removed.

In Bermudas and the Bahamas there is an actual increase.

In Montserrat there is much the same decrease as there has been in Jamaica, which is to be accounted for by the emigrations from that island.

Such, Sir, is the state of the negroes in our West India islands; and it is not only founded upon authentic documents from thence,

thence, but it is alfo confirmed by a variety of other proofs. Mr. Long, whofe works are looked up to in the iflands as a fort of Weft India Gofpel upon thefe fubjects, lays it down as a principle, that when there are two negroes upon an ifland to three hogf-heads of fugar, the work for them will be fo moderate, as to enfure a natural increafe ; and there is now much more than this pro-portion. It can be proved too, that a va-riety of individuals, by good ufage, have more than kept up their ftock.

But, allowing even the number of negroes to be deficient, ftill there are many other refources to be had—the wafte of labour which now prevails—the introduction of the plough and other machinery—the divifion of work, which in free and civilized coun-tries, is the grand fource of wealth—the re-duction of the number of negro fervants, of whom not lefs than from 20 to 40 are kept in ordinary families.—All thefe I touch up-on merely as hints, to fhew that the Weft Indies are not bercaved of, all the means of cultivating their eftates, as fome perfons

.have-

have feared. But, Sir, even if thefe fuppo-
fitions are all falfe and idle, if every one of
thefe fuccedania fhould fail, I ftill do main-
tain, that the Weft India planters can and
will indemnify themfelves by the increafed
price of their produce in our market; a principle which is fo clear, that in queftions of
taxation, or any other queftion of policy,
this fort of argument would undoubtedly
be admitted.

I fay, therefore, that the Weft Indians,
who contend againft the abolition, are non-
fuited in every part of the argument.

Do they fay that importations are neceffary? I have fhewn that the very numbers
in the gang may be kept up by procreation.
Is this denied? I fay, the plough, horfes,
machinery, domeftic flaves, and all the
other fuccedania will fupply the deficiency.
Is it perfifted that the deficiency can in no
way be fupplied, and that the quantity of
produce muft diminifh? I then revert to that
irrefragable argument, that the increafe of
price will make up their lofs, and is a clear
ultimate fecurity.

C   I have

I have in my hand the Extract from a pamphlet, which ftates, in very dreadful colours, what thoufands and tens of thoufands will be ruined; how our wealth will be impaired; one third of our commerce cut off for ever; how our manufactures will droop in confequence, our land-tax be raifed, our marine deftroyed, while France, our natural enemy, and rival, will ftrengthen herfelf by our weaknefs. [A cry of affent being heard from feveral parts of the Houfe, Mr. Wilberforce added,) I beg, Sir, that Gentlemen will not miftake me. The pamphlet, from which this prophecy is taken, was written by Mr. Glover in 1774, on a very different occafion—and I would therefore afk Gentlemen, whether it is indeed fulfilled? Is our wealth decayed? our commerce cut off? our manufactures and our marine deftroyed? Is France raifed upon our ruins?——On the contrary, do we not fee, by the inftance of this pamphlet, how men in a defponding moment will picture to themfelves the moft gloomy confequences, from caufes by no means to be apprehended. We are all, perhaps, in this refpect, apt fometimes to be carried away
by

by a frightened imagination—Like the poor
negroes, we are all, in our turn, fubject to
Obiha; and when we have an intereft to
bias us, we are carried away ten thoufand
times the more.

The African merchants told us laft year,
that if lefs than two men to a ton were to
be allowed, the trade could not continue.
Mr. Tarleton, inftructed by the whole trade
of Liverpool, declared the fame; told us
that commerce would be ruined, and our
manufactures would migrate to France.—
We have petitions on the table from the
manufacturers, but, I believe, they are not
dated at Havre, or any port in France; and
yet it is certain, that, out of twenty fhips
laft year from Liverpool, not lefs than thirteen carried this ruinous proportion of lefs
than two to a ton.

It is faid that Liverpool will be undone—
the trade, fays Mr. Dalziel, at this time
hangs upon a thread, and the fmalleft matter will overthrow it.

I be-

I believe, indeed, the trade hangs upon a thread ; for it is a lofing trade to Liverpool at this time. It is a lottery, in which fome men have made large fortunes, chiefly by being their own infurers, while others follow the example of a few lucky adventurers, and lofe money by it. It is abfurd to fay, therefore, that Liverpool will be ruined by the abolition, or that it will feel the difference very fenfibly, fince the whole outward-bound tonnage of the Slave Trade amounts only to 1-fifteenth of the outward bound tonnage of Liverpool.—We ought to remember alfo, that the Slave Trade actually was fufpended during fome years of the war ; nor did any calamity follow from it.

As to fhipping, our fifheries and other trades will furnifh fo many innocent and bloodlefs ways of employing veffels, that no mifchief need be dreaded from this quarter.

The next fubject which I fhall touch upon, is, the influence of the Slave Trade on our *marine* ; and, inftead of being a benefit to our failors, as fome have ignorantly argued, I do affert it is their . The *grave*

3   evidence

evidence upon the point is clear; for, by
the indefatigable induſtry, and public ſpirit of Mr. Clarkſon, the muſter rolls of all
the ſlave ſhips have been collected and com-
pared with thoſe of other trades; and it
appears, in the reſult, that more ſailors
die in one year in the Slave Trade, than die
in two years in all our other trades put together.

It appears, by the muſter rolls, to 88
ſlave ſhips which ſailed from Liverpool in
1787, that the original crews conſiſted of
3170 ſailors—of theſe only 1428 returned :
642 died, or were loſt, and 1100 were diſ-
charged on the voyage, or deſerted, either
in Africa, or the Weſt-Indies. It appeared
to me for a long time unaccountable, how
ſo vaſt a proportion of theſe ſailors ſhould
leave their ſhips in the Weſt Indies; but I
ſhall quote here a letter from Governor
Parry at Barbadoes, which explains this difficulty :

Extract

Extract of a letter from Governor Parry, to Lord Sydney, dated May 13, 1788, *tranfmitting two Petitions.*

· " To. the African trade on the coaft I cannot venture to fpeak, not being fufficiently acquainted with it ; but am fearful fuch monftrous abufes have crept into it, as to make the interference of the Britifh Legiflature abfolutely neceffary ; and have to lament, that it falls to my lot to poffefs your Lordfhip with the unpleafing information contained in the enclofed petitions, which is fully demonftrative of the fhameful practices carried on in that unnatural commerce."

He then fpeaks of having feen Captain Bibby, who is the perfon mentioned in the following petitions, though the other Captain had endeavoured to prevent it ; and, he fays, he has fent back the pawns (mentioned alfo in the petitions) to their enraged parents—adding, " That I cannot help having my fufpicions ; and I was yefterday told, that he had private inftructions from the petitioners not to prefent the petitions

to

to me, if Bibby would quietly refign the
Pawns; which leads me to believe there
was a general combination in thefe unwar-
rantable practices, among all the mafters of
the veffels then in Cameroons river."

He then comes to the fubject of the Britifh failors—" Your Lordfhip (fays he)
is perfectly informed of the nefarious practices of the African trade, and the cruel
manner in which the greater number of the
mafters treat their feamen. There is fcarce-
ly a veffel in that trade that calls at Barbadoes, from which I have not a complaint
made to me, either by the mafter or the
feamen; but more frequently the latter,
who are often fhamefully ufed; for the African traders at home, being obliged to fend
out their fhips very ftrong handed, as well
from the unhealthinefs of the climate, as
the neceffity of guarding the Slaves, foon
feel the expence of feamen's wages; and as
foon as they come amongft thefe iflands,
and all danger of infurrection is removed,
the mafters quarrel with their feamen, upon the moft frivolous pretences, and turn
them on fhore on the firft ifland they ftop

C 4

at,

at, fometimes with, and fometimes without paying them their wages; and Barbadoes being the windward ftation, has generally a large propoition of thefe men thrown in upon her; and forry am I to fay, that many of thefe valuable fubjects are, from ficknefs, and the dire neceffity of entering into foreign employ for maintenance, loft to the Britifh nation."

Thus do we fee how Mr. Clarkfon's account of the mufter-rolls is verified, and why it is that fo vaft a proportion of failors in the flave fhips is loft to this country.— But let us touch alfo on the petitions which Governor Parry fpeaks of. It feems that the Captain Bibby before mentioned had carried off from Africa thirty of the King's children and relations, left in pawn with him, who retaliated by feizing five Englifh Captains. Thefe Captains difpatch a veffel with petitions to Governor Parry, to fend back the King's fons, in order to their own releafe.— Now, Sir, let us mark the ftile of thefe petitions—" I James M'Gauty,—I William Willoughby, &c. being on fhore on the execution of our bufinefs, were feized by a body

body of armed natives, who lay in ambush
in order to take us."—What villains muſt
theſe Africans be, to ſeize ſo deſignedly ſuch
friends as the. Britiſh ſubjects, and this
merely with a view to get back their own
children !——" This," ſays the petition,
" they effected, and dragged us to their
town, where they treated us in a moſt ſavage and barbarous manner, and loaded us
with irons."—Obſerve, Sir, the indignant
ſpirit of theſe Captains—Britiſh freemen to
be loaded with irons ! White men in cuſto-
dy to theſe barbarous Negroes !—But what
was the cauſe of this abominable outrage ?
" On account," ſay they, " of the *impru-
dent* behaviour of Captain Robert Bibby"—
But what was the *imprudence ?*—" who
carried off thirty pawns, who were the King
and traders' ſons, daughters, and relations."
——Here, then, we have a picture of the
equitable ſpirit in which this trade is carried
on.—Theſe Princes and Chiefs, who, by
Captain Bibby's *imprudence,* had loſt all
their families and children, propoſe, however, to ſatisfy every demand, and to give
theſe Captains their liberty, provided only
they may have their children back again.—

But

But, fay two of the Captains, " We, find-
ing that we could not comply with their
extravagant conditions, did endeavour to re-
gain our liberty, which we effected. But
we verily believe, that our refpective voyages are entirely ruined, the natives being
determined to make no further trade with
either of us, nor pay the above debts, until their fons, daughters, &c. are returned, and debarring us of wood, water, or
any country provifions; therefore we fhall
be forced to leave the river immediately,
and, on that account, we think our voyages
ruined, as before."

It has been urged by fome perfons, in
proof of the *wicked barbarity* of thefe Kings
and Chiefs, that they pawn their own children; from which it is concluded, that
they feel no fort of affection for them, and
therefore deferve all the evils which we in-
flict upon them.

The contrary is in truth the cafe; for the
Captains, knowing the affection they have
for their relations, are willing to take them
as hoftages for very confiderable debts, and

are

are fenfible of their *ideal* value, though the *real* value is trifling; and the fcene which I have juft laid before you very fairly fhews both the general fpirit of our Captains, and the wretched fituation to which our commerce has reduced thefe African Princes :— And if, Sir, at the very moment when Parliament was known to be enquiring into this trade, thefe abufes are thus boldly perfifted in, how can we fuppofe that any regulations, or any palliatives, can overcome thefe enormities, and juftify our continuance of the trade ?—It is true, the African Committee hear little of the matter :—for we find, that even thefe Captains, who were in prifon, inftructed the bearer of their petition, not to apply to Governor Parry, except in the laft neceffity, but merely to get back the King's fons, meaning quietly to compromife matters with Captain Bibby; and if it were not for the vigilance of Governor Parry, the truth would never have come out. In like manner, we find, that although very few failors, when they come to Liverpool, go into an expenfive profecution of their Captains, yet Governor Parry hears of complaints againft them eve-

ry

ry day; and we find, that Juſtice Otley, in the iſland of St. Vincent's, where law is cheap, both hears their grievances, and re-dreſſes them.

There is one other argument, in my opi-nion a very weak and abſurd one, which many perſons, however, have much dwelt upon—I mean, that, if we relinquiſh the ſlave trade, France will take it up.—If the ſlave trade be ſuch as I have deſcribed it, and if the Houſe is alſo convinced of this—if it be in truth both wicked and impolitic, we cannot wiſh a greater miſchief to France than that ſhe ſhould adopt it.—For the ſake of France, however, and for the ſake of humanity, I truſt—nay, I am ſure—ſhe will not. France is too enlightened a na-tion, to begin puſhing a ſcandalous as well as ruinous traffic, at the very time when England ſees her folly, and reſolves to give it up. It is clearly no argument whatever againſt the *wickedneſs* of the trade, that France will adopt it :—For thoſe who ar-gue thus may argue equally, that we may rob, murder, and commit any crime, which any one elſe would have committed, if we

did

did not.—The truth is, that, by our example, we fhall produce the contrary effect.
If we refufe the abolition, we fhall lie,
therefore, under the twofold guilt, of know-
ingly perfifting in this wicked trade ourfelves, and, as far as we can, of inducing France
to do the fame.—Let us, therefore, lead
the way—let this enlightened country take
precedence in this noble caufe, and we fhall
foon find that France is not backward to
follow, nay, perhaps, to accompany our
fteps.—If they fhould be mad enough to
adopt it, they will have every difadvantage
to contend with—They muft buy the negroes much dearer than we; the manufactures they fell muft probably be ours; an
expenfive floating factory, ruinous to the
health of failors, which we have hitherto
maintained muft be fet up; and, after all,
the trade can ferve only as a fort of Gib-
raltar, upon which they may fpend their
ftrength, while the productive branches of
their commerce muft in proportion be neglected and ftarved.

But I have every ground for believing
that the French will not be thus wicked and
abfurd;

abſurd; Mr. Neckar, the enlightened mi-
niſter of that country, a man who has introduced moral and religious principles into
Government, more than has been common
with many miniſters, has actually recorded
his abhorrence of the Slave Trade; he has
under his own hand in his publication on the
finances* pledged himſelf, as it were, to the

* Extract from Mr. Neckeɪ's Treatiſe on the Adminiſtra-
tion of the Finances of France. Vol. 1. ch. 13.

The Colonies of France contain as we have ſeen, near five
hundred thouſand Slaves, and it is from the number of thoſe
wretches, that the inhabitants ſet a value on their Plantations.
What a fatal proſpect! and how profound a ſubject for reflection!—Alas! how inconſequent we are both in our mo-
rality, and our pɪinciples. We preach up humanity, and yet
go every Year to bind in chains twenty thouſand natives of
Afɪica! We call the Moors baɪbarians and ruffians, becauſe
they attack the liberty of Europeans, at the riſk of their own;
yet theſe Europeans go, without danger, and as meɪe ſpecu-
lators to purchaſe ſlaves, by gratifying the cupidity of their
maſteɪs, and excite all thoſe bloody ſcenes which aɪe the
uſual preliminaɪies of this traffick! In ſhoɪt, we pride ourſelves on the ſuperioɪity of man, and it is with reaſon we
diſcover the ſuperiority in the wonderful and myſterious
unfolding of the intellectual faculties; and yet a trifling dif-
feɪence in the hair of the head, or in the colour of the epi-
dermis, is ſufficient to change our reſpect into contempt, and
to engage us to place Beings, like ourſelves, in the rank of
thoſe animals, devoid of reaſon, whom we ſubject to the
yoke, that we may make uſe of their ſtrength and of their
inſtinct at command.

abolition

abolition; and it is impoffible that a man can
be fo loft to all fenfe of decency, and common confiftency of character, as not to forward by every influence in his power, a
caufe in which he has fo publicly declared
himfelf. There is another anecdote which
I mention here with pleafure, which is, that
the King of France very lately being re-
quefted to diffolve a fociety fet up in France,
for the abolition of the Slave Trade, made
anfwer, " that he certainly fhould not, for
that he was very glad it exifted."

I believe, Sir, I have now touched upon
all the objections of any confequence, which
are made to the abolition of this Trade.—
When we confider the vaftnefs of the Continent of Africa; when we reflect how all
other countries have for fome centuries paft,
been advancing in happinefs and civilization;
when we think how in this fame period all
improvement in Africa has been defeated
by her intercourfe with Britain; when we
reflect how it is we ourfelves that have de-
graded them to that wretched brutifhnefs
and barbarity which we now plead as the
juftification of our guilt; how the S lav
Trade

Trade has *enflaved their minds*, blackened their character and funk them fo low in the fcale of animal beings, that fome think the very apes are of a higher clafs, and fancy the *Ourang Outang* has given them the go-by.— What a mortification muft we feel at having fo long neglected to think of our guilt, or to attempt any reparation : It feems, indeed, as if we had determined to forbear from all interference until the meafure of our folly and wickednefs was fo full and complete; until the impolicy which eventually belongs to vice, was become fo plain and glaring, that not an individual in the country fhould refufe to join in the abolition : It feems as if we had waited until the perfons moft intereſted fhould be tired out with the folly and nefarioufnefs of the trade, and fhould unite in petitioning againft it.

Let us then make fuch amends as we can for the mifchiefs we have done to that unhappy Continent : Let us recollect what Europe itfelf was no longer ago than three or four centuries. What if I fhould be able to fhew this Houfe that in a civilized part of Europe, in the time of our Henry II. there

were

were people who actually fold their own children ? what, if I fhould tell them, that England itfelf was that country ? what if I fhould point out to them that the very place where this inhuman traffic was carried on was *the City of Briftol?* Ireland at that time ufed to drive a confiderable trade in flaves, with thefe neighbouring barbarians ; but a great plague having infefted the country, the Irifh were ftruck with a panic, fufpected (I am fure very properly) that the plague was a punifhment fent from Heaven, for the fin of the Slave Trade, and therefore abolifhed it. All I ask, therefore, of the people of Briftol, is, that they would become as civilized now, as Irifhmen were four hundred years ago. Let us put an end at once to this inhuman traffic,—let us ftop this effufion of human blood. The true way to virtue is by withdrawing from temptation;-- let us then withdraw from thefe wretched Africans, thofe temptations to fraud, violence, cruelty, and injuftice, which the Slave Trade furnifhes. Wherever the fun fhines, let us go round the world with him diffufing our beneficence ; but let us not traffic, only that we may fet Kings againft

D

their

their Subjects, Subjects againſt their Kings, ſowing diſcord in every village, fear and terror in every family, ſetting millions of our fellow creatures a hunting each other for ſlaves, creating fairs and markets for human fleſh, through one whole continent of the world, and under the name of policy, concealing from ourſelves all the baſeneſs and iniquity of ſuch a traffic.

Why may we not hope, ere long, to ſee Hans-towns eſtabliſhed on the coaſt of Africa, as they were on the Baltic? It is ſaid the Afiicans are idle, but they are not too idle at leaſt to catch one another: ſeven hundred to one thouſand tons of rice are annually bought of them; by the ſame rule, why ſhould we not buy more: at Gambia one thouſand of them are ſeen continually at work: Why ſhould not ſome more thouſands be ſet to work in the ſame manner? It is the Slave Trade that cauſes their idleneſs, and every other miſchief. We are told by one witneſs, " they ſell one another as they can;" and while they can get brandy by catching one another, no wonder they are too idle for any regular work.

I have

I have one word more to add upon a moſt material point ; but it is a point ſo ſelf evident, that I ſhall be extremely ſhort.

It will appear, from every thing which I have ſaid, that it is not regulation, it is not mere palliatives, that can cure this enormous evil :—Total abolition is the only poſſible cure for it.—The Jamaica report, indeed, admits much of the evil, but recommends it to us, ſo to regulate the trade, that no perſons ſhould be kidnapped or made ſlaves *contrary to the cuſtom of Africa.* But may they not be made ſlaves *unjuſtly,* and yet by no means *contrary to the cuſtom of Africa ?* I have ſhewn they may ; for all the cuſtoms of Africa are rendered ſavage and unjuſt through the influence of this trade : beſides how can we diſcriminate between the ſlaves juſtly and unjuſtly made ? Can we know them by phyſiognomy ? or, if we could, does any man believe that the Britiſh Captains can, by any regulation in this country, be prevailed upon to refuſe all ſuch ſlaves as have not been fairly, honeſtly, and uprightly enſlaved ? But granting even that they ſhould do this, yet how would the

D 2

re-

rejected flaves be recompenfed ? They are brought, as we are told, from three or four thoufand miles off, and exchanged like cattle from one hand to another, until they reach the coaft. We fee then that it is the exiftence of the Slave Trade that is the fpring of all this internal traffic, and that the remedy cannot be applied without abolition. Again, as to the middle paffage, the evil is radical there alfo ; the Merchants profit depends upon the number that can be crouded together, and upon the fhortnefs of their allowance : Aftringents, cicaroticks, and all the other arts of making them up for fale, are of the very effence of the trade ; thefe arts will be concealed both from the purchafer and the legiflature ; they are neceffary to the owner's profit, and they will be practifed. Again, chains and arbitrary treatment muft be ufed in tranfporting them ; our feamen muft be taught to play the tyrant, and that depravation of manners among them (which fome very judicious perfons have treated of, as the very worft part of this bufinefs) cannot be hindered while the trade itfelf continues.

As

As to the flave merchants, they have already told you, that if two flaves to a ton are not permitted, the trade cannot continue; fo that the objections are done away by themfelves on this quarter; and in the Weft Indies, I have fhewn that the abolition is the only poffible ftimulus whereby a regard to population, and confequently to the happinefs of the negroes, can be effectually excited in thofe iflands.

I truft, therefore, I have fhewn, that upon every ground, the total abolition ought to take place. I have urged many things which are not my own leading motives for propofing it, fince I have wifhed to fhew every defcription of Gentlemen, and particularly the Weft India planters, who deferve every attention, that the abolition is politic upon their own principles alfo.

Policy, however, Sir, is not my principle, and I am not afhamed to fay it. There is a principle above every thing that is political; and when I reflect on the command which fays, " *Thou fhalt do no murder,*" believing the authority to be divine, how can

I dare

I dare to fet up any reafonings of my own againft it? And, Sir, when we think of eternity, and of the future confequences of all human conduct, what is there in this life that fhould make any man contradict the dictates of his confcience, the principles of juftice, the laws of religion, and of God.

Sir, the nature and all the circumftances of this trade are now laid open to us; we can no longer plead ignorance,—we cannot evade it,—it is now an object placed before us,—we cannot pafs it; we may fpurn it, we may kick it out of our way, but we cannot turn afide fo as to avoid feeing it; for it is brought now fo directly before our eyes, that this Houfe muft decide, and muft juftify to all the world, and to their own confciences, the rectitude of the grounds and principles of their decifion.

A Society has been eftablifhed for the abolition of this trade, in which Diffenters, Quakers, Churchmen—in which the moft confcientious of all perfuafions have all united, and made a common caufe in this great queftion.

queftion. Let not Parliament be the only body that is infenfible to the principles of national juftice. Let us make reparation to Africa, fo far as we can, by eftablifhing a trade upon true commercial principles, and we fhall foon find the rectitude of our con- duct rewarded, by the benefits of a regular and a growing commerce.

I fhall now move the feveral Refolutions, upon which I do not afk the Houfe to de- cide to-night, but fhall confider the debate as adjourned to any day next week that may be thought moft convenient.

RESOLUTIONS.

I.

THAT the number of flaves annually carried from the coaft of Africa, in Britifh veffels, is fuppofed to be about   38,000

That the number annually carried to the Britifh Weft India Iflands, has (on an average of four years, to the year 1787 inclufive) amounted to about   —   22,500

That

That the number annually retained in the faid Iflands, as far as appears by the Cuftom Houfe accounts, has amounted, on the fame average, to about, — — 17,500

II.

THAT much the greater number of the negroes, carried away by European veffels, are brought from the interior parts of the continent of Africa, and many of them from a very great diftance.

That no precife information appears to have been obtained of the manner in which thefe perfons have been made flaves.

But that from the accounts, as far as any have been procured on this fubject, with refpect to the flaves brought from the interior parts of Africa, and from the information which has been received refpecting the countries nearer to the coaft, the flaves may in general be claffed under fome of the following defcriptions :

1ft. Prifoners taken in war.

2d. Free perfons fold for debt, or on account of real or imputed crimes, particularly adultery and witchcraft ; in which cafes they are frequently fold with their whole families, and fometimes for the profit of thofe by whom they are condemned.

3d. Do-

3d. Domeſtic ſlaves ſold for the profit of their maſters; in ſome places at the will of the maſters, and in ſome places, on being condemned for real or imputed crimes.

4th. Perſons made ſlaves by various acts of op-preſſion. violence, or fraud, committed either by the Princes and Chiefs, of thoſe countries on their ſubjects, or by private individuals on each other; or, laſtly, by Europeans engaged in this traffic.

III.

THAT the trade carried on by European na-tions on the coaſt of Africa, for the purchaſe of ſlaves, has neceſſarily a tendency to occaſion · fre-quent and cruel wars among the natives, to pro-duce unjuſt convictions and puniſhments for pre-tended or aggravated crimes, to encourage acts of oppreſſion, violence and fraud, and to obſtruct the natural courſe of civilization and improvements in thoſe countries.

IV,

THAT the continent of Africa, in its preſent ſtate, furniſhes ſeveral valuable articles of com-merce highly important to the trade and manu-factures of this kingdom, and which are in a great meaſure peculiar to that quarter of the globe; and

(1)   that

that the foil and climate have been found, by experience, well adapted to the production of other articles, with which we are now either wholly, or in great part, supplied by foreign nations.

That an extensive commerce with Africa in these commodities, might probably be substituted in the place of that which is now carried on in slaves, so as at least to afford a return for the same quantity of goods as has annually been carried thither in British vessels.

And, lastly, That such a commerce might reasonably be expected to increase in proportion to the progress of civilization and improvement on that continent.

V.

THAT the Slave Trade has been found, by experience, to be peculiarly injurious and destructive to the British seamen who have been employed therein ; and that the mortality among them has been much greater than in his Majesty's ships stationed on the coast of Africa, or than has been usual in British vessels employed in any other trade.

VI.

THAT the mode of transporting the slaves from Africa to the West Indies necessarily exposes them

to

to many and grievous fufferings, for which no regulation can provide an adequate remedy; and
that, in confequence thereof, a large proportion
of them has annually perifhed during the voyage.

VII.

THAT a large proportion of the flaves fo tranf-
ported, has alfo perifhed in the harbours in the Weft
Indies previous to their being fold. That this
lofs is ftated by the affembly of the Ifland of Jamaica at about four and a half per. cent. of the
number imported; and is, by medical perfons of
experience in that Ifland, afcribed, in great meafure, to difeafes contracted during the voyage, and
to the mode of treatment on board the fhips, by
which thofe difeafes have been fuppreffed for a
time, in order to render the flaves fit for immediate fale.

VIII.

THAT the lofs of newly imported Negroes, within the firft three years after their importation, bears
a large proportion to the whole number imported.

IX.

THAT the natural increafe of population,
among the Slaves in the iflands, appear to have
been impeded principally by the following caufes:

1ft.

ıft. The inequality of the number of the fexes, in the importations from Africa.

2d. The general diffolutenefs of manners among, the Slaves, and the want of proper regulations for the encouragement of marriages, and of rearing children.

3d. Particular difeafes which are prevalent a-mong them, and which are in fome inftances attri-buted to too fevere labour or rigorous treatment; and in others to infufficient or improper food.

4th. Thofe difeafes which affect a large propor-tion of Negro children in their infancy, and thofe to which the Negroes newly imported from Africa have been found to be particularly liable.

X.

THAT the whole number of Slaves in the ifland of Jamaica, in 1768, was about — — — — 167,000;

THAT the number in 1774, was fta-ted by Governor Keith, about — 193,000;

And, that the number in December 1787, as ftated by Lieutenant Governor Clarke, was about — — . 256,000.

That,

That, by comparing thefe number with the numbers imported into and retained in the ifland, in the feveral years from 1768 to 1774 inclufive, as appearing from the accounts delivered to the committee of trade by Mr. Fuller ; and in the feveral years from 1775 inclufive, to 1787 alfo inclufive, as appearing by the accounts delivered in by the Infpector General ; and allowing for a lofs of about one twenty fecond part by deaths on fhip-board after entry, as ftated in the Report of the Affembly of the faid Ifland of Jamaica, it appears,

That the annual excefs of deaths above births in the Ifland in the whole period of nineteen years, has been in the proportion of about feven eighths per cent. computing on the medium number of Slaves in the Ifland during that period.

That in the firft fix years of the faid nineteen, the excefs of deaths was in the proportion of rather more than one on every hundred on the medium number.

That in the laft thirteen years of the faid nineteen, the excefs of deaths was in the proportion of about three-fifths on every hundred on the medium number; and that a number of Slaves, amounting to 15,000, is ftated by the report of the ifland of Jamaica to have perifhed, during the latter period in confequence of repeated hurricanes, and of the want of foreign fupplies of provifions.

XI.

XI.

That the whole number of Slaves in the ifland of Barbadoes was, in the year 1764, according to the account given in to the Committee of Trade by Mr. Braithwaite, — — — 70,706

That in 1774, the number was, by the fame account — — 74,874

In 1780, by ditto — — 68,270

In 1781, after the hurricane, according to the fame account — — — 63,248

In 1786, by ditto — — 62,115

That by comparing thefe numbers with the number imported into this ifland, according to the fame account, (not allowing for any re-exportation) the annual excefs of deaths, above births, in the ten years from 1764 to 1774, was in the proportion of about five on every hundred, computing on the medium number of Slaves in the ifland during that period.

That in the feven years from 1774 to 1780, both inclufive, the excefs of deaths was in the proportion of about one and one-third on every hundred, on the medium number.

That between the year 1780 and 1781, there appears to have been a decreafe in the number of Slaves of about 5,000.

I

That

(63)

That in the fix yeais from 1781 to 1786, both inclufive, the excefs of deaths was in the proportion of rather lefs than feven-eighths in every hundred, on the medium number.

And that in the four years from 1783 to 1786, both inclufive, the excefs of deaths was in the proportion of rather lefs than one-third in every hundred, on the medium number.

And that during the whole period, there is no doubt that fome were exported fiom the ifland, but confiderably moie in the firft part of this period than in the laft.

XII.

THAT the accounts from the Leeward Iflands, and from Dominica, Grenada, and Saint Vincent's ; do not furnifh fufficient grounds for comparing the ftate of population in the faid Iflands at different periods, with the number of Slaves which have been from time to time imported into the faid Iflands, and exported therefrom.

But that, from the evidence which has been received refpecting the prefent ftate of thefe Iflands, as well as of Jamaica and Barbadoes, and from a confideration of the means obviating the caufes which have hitherto operated to impede the natural
increafe

increafe of the Slaves, and of leffening the demand
for manual labour, without diminifhing the profit
of the planter, it appears that no confiderable or
permanent inconvenience would refult from difcon-
tinuing the farther importation of African Slaves.

N. B. It is the intention after paffing thefe refolutions, to move for leave to bring in a bill for the
total abolition of the Slave Trade.

LORD PENRHYN,

After a tribute of approbation to the
beauty, force, and eloquence of what Mr.
Wilberforce had juft delivered, faid, he
fhould indeed appear but with an ill grace ;
yet was he fo firmly fixed in his opinion of
the mifchiefs which an unqualified abolition
of the flave trade muft occafion, that he
found it his duty to oppofe the main point
of the Honourable Gentleman's argument.
He did fo from a pre-conviction—he did fo
from the errors—palpable errors to be found
in the reports, fpeeches, and quotations al-
luded

luded to, moſt of which were either mis-
ſtated or miſapplied. A regulation might
be requiſite; but a total abolition was going a ſtep beyond the bounds of prudence
or rectitude.

Mr. BAMBER GASCOYNE,

On the ſame ſide of the argument, contended, that a total unqualified abolition would
do an injury to private property and to
public intereſt. The Honourable Gentleman, who had his plan ſo near at heart,
gave the Committee a very fine ſyſtem of
agriculture, which country gentlemen, who
underſtood the plough, might conceive well
adapted to this country; but how it applied
to the burning regions of the weſt, was yet
to be proved. He then entered into a de-
fence of what he ſaid laſt year on the ſubject of tonnage, which he contended was
now mis-ſtated by the Honourable Gentleman; and, as to the loſs of ſeamen, he
would take upon him to aver, that, inſtead
of a check to the African ſlave trade ſerving
our marine, it did them the moſt eſſentia

E   inj

injury, numbers being at this moment in want of bread, on account of the bill passed in the last Session of Parliament, for the regulation of tonnage. He did not wish to give a hasty opinion on the business, and therefore requested, that time might be allowed for confideration of the subject, on the calculations made in the Honourable Gentleman's speech; and he trusted, when this fairness was adopted, and the warmth of prejudice removed, that the African flave trade would be found productive of a confiderable revenue to this country.

Mr. WILBERFORCE

Affured the House, that he had not *wilfully* mis-ftated the matter. He might err, but it was not with the confent of his mind; for he really believed every fyllable he had uttered to be ftrictly founded on truth. He begged it might be so underftood, that he did not mean to bring the fubject into debate on its broad bafis at prefent.—He wifhed to give time for a due confideration of the fubject; and therefore, if

it

it was agreeable to the Committee, fhould mention Monday as a proper day to go into the difcuffion of the feveral motions which were offered to the Committee.

Mr. BURKE.

Gave his opinion on the fubject.—It was, that the flave trade fhould be totally abolifhed.—It was a difgrace to human nature—it began in murderous war—it ended in perpetual exile ; and what aggravated the fcene of horror was, that the unhappy fufferers were not known to be guilty of any crime whatfoever. He was againft going at all into thofe merits contained in the papers which the Honourable Gentleman had laid upon the table. His idea was, that the motion fhould now be made for a total abolition of this inhuman traffic ; fo that, in procefs of time, commerce might extend itfelf over the vaft continent of Africa, as well as in the more narrowed and civilized parts of Europe. But however he coincided in the general idea with the Honourable Gentleman, yet he could not heartily

E 2   agree

agree in the mode by which the purport of
that idea was to be fulfilled. He wifhed
for no abftracted queftions, but to come at
once to the point ; for each motion, as now
read to the Houfe, might occafion debate, and
that debate produce, *poffibly*, he would not fay
probably, a caufe to fight a word out ; and
if it fhould, by any misfortune, be the
means of putting a negative upon the whole,
the matter would appear as a difgrace upon
the journals of Parliament. Hence he recom-
mended brevity, and advifed that the motion
fhould contain no more than a refolution of
the Committee, that the flave trade fhould
be totally abolifhed ; to which motion he
fhould give his moft hearty affirmative, on
account of the purity of its principles ; for,
if the bill was thrown out in the Lords,
the refolutions, ftanding on the Journals,
would become a *recorded* cenfure on the
Commons.

Inftead of feeing the unhappy Africans
thus treated by the Sons of Freedom,
he trufted, we fhould inftantly put a
ftop to this evil, and, inftead of counte-
nancing the fale of our fellow creatures,
begin

begin a new kind of traffic, and barter illicit profit for glorious humanity. His reafon for troubling the Houfe at prefent, was,
that his duty in another place, might, in
all probability, make it impoffible for him
to attend on Monday next, and, therefore,
what fentiments he had to offer, he then
wifhed to deliver. He paid many compli-
ments to Mr. Wilberforce for what he faid,
and declared, that it might be truly called
one of the beft fpeeches ever delivered in
Parliament, in favour of a race of beings
who had this fole comfort, that the *Slave*
was only compenfated by not being a *Man.*

Mr. P I T T

Could not permit fo important a matter
to pafs without faying a few words. He
gave his moft hearty concurrence to all that
had been fo eloquently fpoken by his Honourable Friend, and was fully convinced
in his own mind, that there fhould be a
*total and unqualified repeal of the Slave Trade
Law.* He differed with Mr. Burke as to
his idea refpecting the motion; becaufe he
thought that nothing fhort of uncondition-
ally

ally abolishing the whole of this traffic, could be of service to the cause of humanity. The House, he therefore trusted, would cordially concur in one opinion, and he wished, for the honour of Britain, it might be an unanimous vote on the occasion. As to France, he trusted, from every matter he could learn, that she would be content to follow our plan of emancipation, when she found she could not take the lead in so glorious a business.

He said it was, indeed, a momentous question, and that nothing but its not being truly understood, could ever have prevented its being hitherto adopted. However, he had no doubt of this great question being at last decided by the immutable law of justice, for it was a subject on which truth must and would be invincible. Something had been thrown out respecting the advantage foreign countries might take of our giving up this traffic—but that was idle speculation. Great Britain was always able to prevent an illicit trade of negroes by any other power to the West Indies; but of that

there

there was no great apprehenfion ; the French were probably following up our idea, and, perhaps, meaning to enter into a negociation with us on the fubject.

Mr. F O X

Said, he never had heard a debate with more fatisfaction than the prefent. With regard to the plan of laying the propofitions before the Houfe, where he was agreed as to the fubftance of a meafure, he did not like to differ as to the form of it. If, however, he differed in any thing, it was rather with a view to forward the bufinefs than to injure it, or to throw any thing like an obftacle or impediment in its way. Nothing like either fhould come from him. What he thought was, that all the propofitions were not neceffary to be voted, previous to the ultimate vote, though fome of them undoubtedly were. In order to explain this, he reminded the Honourable Gentleman, that the propofitions were of two forts ; one

fort

fort alleged the fit grounds on which the House ought to proceed to abolifh the Slave Trade, viz. that it was a difgrace to humanity, that it was attended with the lofs of lives to our feamen, as well as the Africans, &c. &c. Another fort contained affertions in anfwer, as it were, to the objections that had been ftated, or were fuppofed likely to be ftated. The putting fuch refolutions on their Journals might create a difficulty to foreign powers; becaufe what might be a matter of objection to Great Britain, might not be fo to any other country.

. Mr. Fox applauded Mr. Wilberforce, and gave him his thanks for profeffing to do what he thought it their duty to do, *viz.* to completely abolifh the traffic in Slaves; a traffic, for continuing which, on no ground, either a plea of policy or neceffity could be urged. Wherever an effectual remedy could not be had, Mr. Fox faid, he approved a palliative, becaufe fomething like a remedy was better, than no remedy at all; in the prefent cafe, an effectual remedy was not only more defirable, but it was much lefs difficult to be obtained that a palliative.

He

He was glad that the Propofitions were to be put upon the Journals ; becaufe if from any misfortune, the bufinefs fhould fail, while it ftood upon the Journals, it might fucceed another year; certain it was, it could not fail to fucceed fooner or later. Foreign countries, when they heard that the matter had been difcuffed in that Houfe, might follow the example, or they might go before us, and fet one themfelves. If this were to happen, though we might be the lofers, humanity would be the gainer.

Mr. Fox reminded the Houfe that he had always been particularly fanguine that whenever they examined the Slave Trade thoroughly, they would find it not only inhuman but impolitic ; from what the Honourable Gentleman, who had fubmitted the Propofitions to their confideration, had faid, it was clear there was as little policy as humanity in the Trade. But what he rofe chiefly for, Mr. Fox faid, was to notice what had fallen from the Right Honourable Gentleman refpecting the probability of foreign nations affuming the Slave Trade on our abandoning it, and,

F.   in

in an illicit manner, fupplying our Weft-
India Iflands with Slaves. He had intended
to have rifen to have faid the very fame
thing, becaufe he was convinced that it
was the fit tone to be held on fuch a fubject,
and that foreign nations might be given to
underftand, that when this country thought
proper to abolifh the Slave trade, we had
refources among us to prevent that Trade
being carried on in any manner with
our Colonies.—With regard to what the
Honourable Gentleman who fpoke laft had
faid, in declaring that a clandeftine trade
in Slaves was worfe than a legal one, he
differed entirely. He thought fuch a trade,
if it exifted at all, fhould be only clandeftine. A trade in human flefh was fo fcan-
dalous, that it was to the laft degree infa-
mous to let it be openly carried on by the
authority of the Government of any country.
Mr. Fox faid, he had fometimes been
thought to ufe too harfh expreffions of
France, in treating her as the rival of this
country.—Politically fpeaking, France certainly was our rival; but he well knew
the diftinction between political enmity and
illiberal prejudice.—If there was any great

2   and

and enlightened nation now exifting in Europe, it was France, which was as likely as any nation on the face of the globe, to act, on the prefent fubject, with warmth and with enthufiafm; to catch a fpark from the light of our fire, and to run a race with us in promoting the ends of humanity.

If France fhould decline to join with us, the honour, indeed would then be all our own—but he thought, however, we ought not to refufe them a participation of this honour, if we could thereby forward the great ends of humanity, and unite them immediately in the fame caufe.

THE SPEAKER

Paid a high compliment to Mr. Wilberforce, and warmly approved of the Abolition.

ALDERMAN NEWNHAM

Was against any Bill of the kind.

Mr.

Mr. DEMPSTER

Enquired whether there was to be a compensation to mortgagees and planters.

Mr. PITT

Said that he did not wish to be understood as pledged for any compensation.

LORD PENRHYN

Accused Mr. Wilberforce of misquoting Mr. Long, and spoke warmly against the Abolition, observing that Seventy Millions of property were involved in this question.

Mr. SMITH.

Said a few words in favour of the Abolition, and the House adjourned.

FINIS.

9 781016 360814